MERCIES
NEW EVERY MORNING

31 Days of Reflection and Meditation

Volume I

EDITED BY KEITH MAGEE
~ FOREWORD DR. ROBIN L. SMITH ~

Published by Keith Magee 2024

Copyright ©Keith Magee 2024

Managing Editor Joanne Clay

Cover Design by Shayan Shaukat

British Library Cataloguing-in-Publication Data
Library of Congress Cataloguing-in-Publication Data

Designed by Dolman Scott

ISBN: 978-1-915351-37-1

Published by

DolmanScott

www.dolmanscott.com

To you, the reader, may you find
inspiration, hope, courage, joy, strength, and love
here within

To the lost and the found

ABBREVIATIONS OF BIBLE TRANSLATIONS

AMP	–	Amplified Bible
ESV	–	English Standard Version
KJV	–	King James Version
NIV	–	New International Version
NKJV	–	New King James Version
NLT	–	New Living Translation
RSV	–	Revised Standard Version
TPT	–	The Passion Translation
WEB	–	World English Bible

CONTENTS

FOREWORD

This is what the Lord says: "Stand at the crossroads and look; ask for the ancient paths, ask where the good way is, and walk in it, and you will find rest for your souls. But you said, 'We will not walk in it.'"
Jeremiah 6:16 (NIV)

The prophet Jeremiah, known as the weeping prophet, emerged in the late 7th and early 6th centuries BCE. Considered a wise, empathic elder with a double-edged message of warning and lament, Jeremiah also highlighted the path of redemption for those lost in distraction, self-centeredness, or faithlessness — calling them back to share in the culture of wholehearted faith. Jeremiah initially felt ill-equipped for his calling, wanting God to find a more noble suitor for what seemed like mission impossible.

Mercies: New Every Morning invites us, with holy fear, awe, and trembling, to embrace anew our divine birthright of being Naked and Unashamed.

Maturing requires making space for all our feelings and thoughts — both the acceptable and those lurking in the shadows. Every part of us calls for a compassionate, curious, and accountable inner world to be examined, challenged, and understood. The sacred and empowering grounds of lament and joy are essential markers on the faith journey.

This collection is written for you — the beloved searcher and seeker, the known and unknown, the claimed and unclaimed. It is for those who have met God and themselves at the intersection of being lost yet still worthy.

Living unshackled is about far more than breaking physical bonds. It means dismantling hatred — both for ourselves and others — and crowning Love as sovereign. True freedom — the kind no one can steal — is about unlocking the chains of conditioning on our hearts and minds. ***Mercies: New Every Morning*** is a practical companion, helping you move away from the dangerous walls that exile you from yourself, your people, and your God. It is an invitation to tear down the barriers that separate you from your brothers and sisters in the human family.

Our elitist insecurities have bred angst, isolation, and loneliness — denying the fundamental truth of all creation: we are all immigrants and refugees on this planet. We are tenants, not owners, living here by grace, not by any mighty works of our own hands. We are visitors. ***Mercies: New Every Morning*** calls us into communion with God, ourselves, and each other.

If you are searching for inspiration, comfort, enlightenment, and unspeakable joy, ***Mercies: New Every Morning*** offers a balm in Gilead — a healing friend for the soul. As you read, ask for the message meant for you in that moment to manifest with simplicity, tenderness, courage, and grace.

This devotional is a personal invitation to seek and embrace more fully your humanity as a traveler of faith, even in seasons when your faith feels fragile, flawed, or yearning for renewal. Bring your holy, holey, and unholy questions to the table, and ask to be met exactly where you are in this moment.

The shattered pieces of your life's magnificent tapestry will find roots and wings within the pages of ***Mercies: New Every Morning***. It is a divine invitation to cast your net again when you've fished all night and caught nothing. It is the call and response that rocks you between seasickness and stillness, helping you speak peace to your storms.

Let's remember: birds don't long to be frogs, and lions don't wish to be giraffes. Only humans struggle with the longing to be something other than themselves. Listening for the *sound of the genuine*, you will encounter the rich world of Both-And, not the narrow limitations of Either-Or. You will explore what it means to win and lose, to be strong and fragile in the same breath, and to find yourself victorious — even when part of the "losing" team.

Michelangelo's painting of the prophet Jeremiah on the Sistine Chapel ceiling captures the complexity not only of the prophet but of every human being — daring to reimagine a new dance and a fresh encounter with hope, possibility, and love.

Mercies: New Every Morning calls you by name, with radical courage, to take your place in this sacred moment. Swing your heart and arms wide open and await the fresh visitation of God in the fierce urgency of now.

Dr. Robin L. Smith

INTRODUCTION

When we stand at the threshold of any kind of change – whether that is a new year, a new life stage or simply the dawn of another day – we are often compelled to reflect, recalibrate, and search for new directions. Such instances offer an opportunity to take stock and ask ourselves how we can better align with God's promise and the purpose He has for us.

In Lamentations 3:22-24 (ESV), the prophet Jeremiah writes:

The steadfast love of the Lord never ceases;
his mercies never come to an end;
they are new every morning;
great is your faithfulness.
"The Lord is my portion," says my soul,
"therefore I will hope in him."

As we navigate the complexities of life – the unexpected detours, the episodes of anguish and of joy – Jeremiah's powerful words remind us of the enduring faithfulness of God. His love never falters, and each day He offers us mercy, grace, and hope to guide us.

Mercies: New Every Morning has been compiled to uplift, inspire, and encourage all who read it to remain unwavering in their faith. Whether you are seeking solace after a tough year, looking for counsel as you step into fresh beginnings, or desiring a deeper connection with the Lord, this book is for you. Each devotion invites you into a space of contemplation and meditation, bringing you closer to the heart of God and helping you experience a renewed sense of optimism.

At the center of this project lies my profound faith in the power of love, prayer, and stillness before God. I believe that by sitting silently, listening intently, and opening our minds to our creator, we can find solutions to life's greatest challenges. One of my guiding philosophies, which resonates throughout this collection, is that justice and Jesus are inextricably linked – because justice is love in action and God is love. In a world often fraught with division, injustice, and pain, I try to always remember that divine love is the answer to the cries of our souls.

Drawn from many different walks of life, the contributors to ***Mercies: New Every Morning*** echo this truth. They offer words of comfort and wisdom that flow from their own encounters with God's grace. Some have faced overwhelming personal difficulties, while others have known the quiet trials of doubt or weariness. Yet all share a common conviction – an abiding faith that God's light shines brightest in our darkest moments.

As you read through this devotional, you will encounter themes of hope, perseverance, and the unchanging nature of God's love. You will be reminded that no matter how overwhelming life may seem, no matter the depth of your struggle or the uncertainty of your future, God's compassion never fails. His mercies – which provide us with the strength and courage to move forward – are bestowed on us anew every morning.

Keith Magee
London, December 2024

A FATHER'S LOVE
By Sharon White

Even if my father and mother abandon me,
the Lord will hold me close.

Psalm 27:10 (NLT)

Some people, through no fault of their own, come from a background that is broken, dysfunctional, or hit by loss, leaving them lacking the loving bonds close kinship can bring. Thankfully, God's care for His children extends far beyond bloodlines – He ensures we can be part of a family created by love. He strategically places individuals in our lives to guide and support us toward spiritual truth, while tending to our emotional wounds.

When my mother was dying, I experienced a rollercoaster of feelings, including anger. How could the Lord take from me the only person who had ever shown me real love? I pleaded with God, telling Him if He was going to take my mother, He needed to send someone to fill the hole that was going to be left in my heart. Not long after, my pastor unexpectedly became that person – the father I never had.

Our relationship has not been without its challenges; it has been as turbulent as that of any natural father and daughter, filled with misunderstandings and disagreements. Yet, despite our ups and downs, we always find our way back to love. This is the same for all of us when it comes to our relationship with the Lord. We don't always get it right, and sometimes find ourselves separating from God. However, His love will always draw us back to Him.

As an administrator in Boston Public Schools, Sharon White thrives on educating children and young people. She believes, as Matthew 6:21 (NIV) tells us, that 'where your treasure is' – meaning the pursuits you value most – 'there your heart will be also.'

A GOOD NAME – OUR SHARED HUMANITY
By Keith Magee

A good name is better than fine perfume.
Ecclesiastes 7:1 (NIV)

Our names carry the weight of our actions, our character, and the way we touch the lives of others. They are more precious than any material wealth because they represent our legacy. In today's culture, it's easy to fall into the trap of labelling and name-calling, reducing someone to a stereotype. Yet, we must be mindful not to let biases cloud our mind's judgment. A good name, rooted in integrity and decency, transcends any lazy cliché.

One of the greatest sources of strength and support along my personal journey is my dear friend Karen. While the name Karen has become stigmatized in popular culture, particularly in Black America, my friend's life proves that labels do not define a person. She has dedicated herself to supporting meaningful social causes – planting seeds of hope and watching them grow. Her commitment to community and fairness is a reminder that we

3

must be careful not to fall into the very traps of bigotry we seek to dismantle.

There are many who are not like us but who stand with us in the fight for justice and equality. We are stronger together when we see beyond the limits of our surface differences and honor the shared pursuits of tolerance, generosity, and love.

As the Torah teaches in Leviticus 19:34 (NIV), '*The foreigner residing among you must be treated as your native-born. Love them as yourself.*' Let us extend loving kindness to all, embracing the unity that comes from our collective humanity.

Keith Magee is an American pastor, professor, and public intellectual who is based in the UK. He lives in the power of love that transcends ethnicity, gender, race, religion, sexuality, and politics.

A PRAYER OF THANKS
By Monica Murray

The steadfast love of the Lord never ceases;
    his mercies never come to an end;
they are new every morning;
    great is your faithfulness.
                    Lamentations 3:22-24 (ESV)

I heard the voice of the Lord say unto me, "Wake up, wake up!" As I arose, I saw the birds chirping at the window, singing sweet melodies unto the creator. I heard Him saying unto me, "This is a new day. It's a day when you shall sing praises unto Me and glorify My name.

"I shall blow a fresh wind upon you. One you have never felt before. You shall dance before Me early in the morning. Singing unto Me like the birds."

Suddenly, it was as though I could sense the Lord's glory. It was much like in Exodus 33:21-23, when Moses couldn't see God's face but knew He was there though His presence. WOW! O what a day of rejoicing it was. My God! O I melted as His anointing fell upon me. I will never be the same again.

Now, whenever I read this scripture, I recognize that kind and loving God. Knowing His mercies never stop, I can expect new mercies day by day. Great is His faithfulness.

Heavenly Father, I thank You for another day's journey. For allowing us to know that You are with us. Lord God, You keep us, strengthen us, direct us, and never leave us. It is Your steadfast love that never ceases or fails us. In Jesus' name. Amen.

A ministry leader in the preached gospel and prayer, Monica Murray resides in Washington, DC, USA. She holds dear the declaration in 2 Corinthians 5:7 that we, 'walk by faith, not by sight,' which aligns with her belief in the power of prayer.

ACCEPT GOD AS YOUR GUIDE EVERY MORNING
By Alexa and Paul Achkar

Let the morning bring me word of your unfailing love,
*   for I have put my trust in you.*
Show me the way I should go,
*   for to you I entrust my life.*

Psalm 143:8 (NIV)

Have you ever woken up overwhelmed with uncertainty and feeling the day ahead is just too big to overcome or too hard to navigate?

As humans, it is a natural part of our existence to shy away from uncertainty. In those early moments of waking, as our minds begin to race with what is ahead of us on any given day, we often neglect to pause and check in with ourselves – and with God.

Psalm 143:8 reminds us there is a different way to approach those mornings when doubt weighs down on us. It's all about perspective. What if, instead of viewing the early morning as a time to endure uncertainty, we saw it as a time to seek guidance? Thanks to God's unfailing love, every morning when you awaken you have the potential to make of that day whatever you want. The words of this psalm invite us into a moment of stillness in which we can take the opportunity to welcome God's love and follow His lead. The commitment here is twofold: God points us toward His chosen path for us, and we accept Him as our guide, deepening our relationship with Him.

When you wake up tomorrow, take a few minutes to invite God into your day. Ask Him to reveal His love to you and show you the way. Make it a daily practice to trust Him with your life – and watch how your perspective transforms.

Alexa and Paul Achkar are a newlywed couple embarking on a shared life and faith together in Manhattan, New York. Alexa channels her creativity through her own design studio, while Paul works in finance at an investment firm.

COUNTING MY BLESSINGS

By Théo Le Douarin

For you created my inmost being;
*   you knit me together in my mother's womb.*
I praise you because I am fearfully and wonderfully
made;
*   your works are wonderful,*
*   I know that full well.*

Psalm 139:13-14 (NIV)

I was born two months before term. Nobody knew why I wanted to be out of my mother's womb even before the designated time. Perhaps it was my calling, perhaps I wanted to breathe the air of earth's marvels.

I grew up in the care of my wonderful parents, my loved ones, and my wider family and friends. And as I transition from childhood to adolescence, each morning I count my blessings as I savor the beauty of God's gift of life.

As a teenager, I have my fears and my insecurities, my faults and my frailties. I have experienced friendships that started as positive and enriching, only to end with bittersweet disappointments. But I embrace these challenges with trust and confidence, knowing that I am blessed with love, peace, and happiness. My family is always there to inspire and guide me. And I have my best friends who will always listen.

I love to write, I love to draw, I love to imagine things, and I love to create. As I write my thoughts about life, I know that I am leaving traces of my own truths. These truths make me strong and powerful. Now, as I reflect on the words of this psalm, they reveal to me God's truth: life is beautiful. I have known it since I was in my mother's womb, and I feel blessed every day.

Théo Le Douarin is a 14-year-old French-Filipino boy who loves to write, draw, listen to music, and play video games. He believes that there is beauty in every culture.

DISCOVERING STRENGTH IN OVERWHELM
By Cyntoria Grant

Hear my cry, O God; attend unto my prayer.

From the end of the earth will I cry unto thee, when my heart is overwhelmed: lead me to the rock that is higher than I.

Psalm 61:1-2 (KJV)

In the seemingly never-ending hustle and bustle of life – juggling home, school, work, and family – it's easy to feel overwhelmed. Your cup may feel full to the brim, and the weight of responsibilities can seem like it is dragging you down. At times like these it's important to remember that you are not alone.

When life becomes too much to bear, take a moment to cry out to God. He hears your pleas and is attentive to your prayers. The assurance that you can reach out from wherever you are, even in the depths of overwhelm, brings comfort. God invites you to turn to Him when your heart feels heavy.

Picture yourself standing on unstable ground. Then remind yourself that in times of uncertainty, God serves as your rock – a steady foundation when everything else feels chaotic. You can find refuge in His presence, where your burdens can be lifted.

Today, take a brief pause to reflect. Lean into God's presence, knowing that He is always with you. Remember that His strength is perfect, especially when you feel weak. Lean on Him and let Him lighten your load.

Cyntoria Grant is an educator, leader, and change agent from Boston, MA, USA. Her life motto is inspired by Maya Angelou: 'Every moment is a teachable moment, so when you learn, teach, and when you get, give, so you leave no one behind.'

EVERYONE IS DESERVING OF YOUR HELP

By Bryan Bonaparte

"'For I was hungry and you gave me something to eat, I was thirsty and you gave me something to drink, I was a stranger and you invited me in, I needed clothes and you clothed me, I was sick and you looked after me, I was in prison and you came to visit me.'

"Then the righteous will answer him, 'Lord, when did we see you hungry and feed you, or thirsty and give you something to drink? When did we see you a stranger and invite you in, or needing clothes and clothe you? When did we see you sick or in prison and go to visit you?'

"The King will reply, 'Truly I tell you, whatever you did for one of the least of these brothers and sisters of mine, you did for me.'"

Matthew 25:35-40 (NIV)

If you thought the stranger in need standing right in front of you was God, how would you treat that person? Would you not do whatever you could to help them without hesitation? Would you not feed them, clothe them, give them money, offer soothing or uplifting words, and show love and care for them in every way possible?

Research shows we are more inclined to help those who look like us. In other words, we are more likely to provide assistance to those with whom we can most easily identify, because we see ourselves reflected in them. Conversely, we are more likely to ignore the plight of people we perceive as being very different from us – we tend to regard them with fear, distrust, and hostility rather than compassion.

I think this scripture goes deeper than Leviticus 19:18 (KJV) '... *love thy neighbour as thyself.*' What this verse from Matthew 25 says to me is that God resides in all of us and therefore we should look for Him in all human beings – especially those in need – and act accordingly. For when we come to the aid of our most desperate 'brothers and sisters' – however dissimilar to us they may appear to be – we are, in fact, helping the Lord.

Bryan Bonaparte is a senior lecturer at the University of Westminster and is based in the UK. He believes you should always treat other people the way you want to be treated.

FINDING GOD IN MOMENTS OF STILLNESS
By Valerie Mosley

He says, "Be still, and know that I am God;
    I will be exalted among the nations,
    I will be exalted in the earth."

                                    Psalm 46:10 (NIV)

In the busyness of life, we are often tossed to and fro: responding to this email, running to catch the train, putting out several fires at once. Technologies, family, and work all call us into action and away from stillness. We can't hear from God if we don't allow the quiet into our lives.

This scripture is a command – an authoritative order that provides immeasurable benefits if we choose to listen.

Being still is a great mindful practice. When we are quiet and still, we can hear the voice of God more loudly. More succinctly. In our stillness is peace. Fear doesn't exist in peace.

Much happens when we are KNOWing; it's a powerful force. Steeped in undeniable confidence, one who knows will do, will try, will rebound. One who knows moves toward the direction of their heart's desire, without doubt. One who knows will make progress even in the presence of doubt.

'That I am God' has two impactful meanings. The first is a reminder that you are not alone and instead are co-partnered with the greatest universal energy – God. Such a knowing is incredibly empowering. The second is that I, you, we are co-creators with God – we have more abilities and gifts than we can ever imagine, and we can use these to create, achieve, and share to positively impact others.

Find the quiet. Find the peace. God is there. And when you hear from God, don't doubt. Instead: Act. Do. Create. Help. Inspire. Press onward. Love.

Chief Visionary Officer for BrightUp, Valerie Mosley lives on Martha's Vineyard in Massachusetts, USA. She is convinced of two important edicts: that your self-worth should not be a function of your net worth, and that there is immense power in unconditional self-love.

FINDING REST IN THE ARMS OF JESUS
By Michael Turton

Come unto me, all ye that labour and are heavy laden, and I will give you rest.

Matthew 11:28 (KJV)

Are you not heavy laden? Do you not feel the weight of your burdens? Are you not weary?

I am. I'm sure you are too. At some times more than others, but it's there. However, there is hope – we can each find help to relieve us of our troubles and exhaustion.

The Bible includes many verses that we can read deeply into. Some are complex and require careful analysis to make their lessons accessible to believers' hearts. But this verse from the gospel of Matthew is direct and relates to all of us. It brings us to the loving arms of Jesus with a very simple instruction: *'Come unto me… .'* It tells us we are not alone in our struggles and there is a way out. A way to find both peace and rest.

Say this prayer and feel the words as you deliver them to God:

"Dear Father in Heaven, my creator and savior. Hear my plea for Your loving arms to take this burden off my shoulders and ease my weary soul. I come to You with little strength and I am asking You for Yours. Draw close to me, Lord, and grace me with Your loving presence to keep me strong in my times of need. In Jesus' mighty name. Amen."

Michael Turton is a surgical technician from Oxford, UK. He came to Christ desperate for peace and rest and, on reading this scripture, found faith and joy.

GOD HAS FAITH IN YOUR ABILITIES
By Keith Magee

"You are braver than you believe, and stronger than you seem, and smarter than you think."
Christopher Robin to Winnie-the-Pooh in *Pooh's Grand Adventure: The Search for Christopher Robin* by Walt Disney Pictures

Winnie-the-Pooh is a collection of stories by British author, AA Milne. The tales are based on the times Milne spent with his young son, Christopher Robin, who would take his favorite stuffed bear with them on walks in the woods. Disney brings the books to life through movies. In *Pooh's Grand Adventure: The Search for Christopher Robin*, knowing he must go to school the next day, Christopher Robin tries to explain to Pooh that the pair will be apart for a while. But Pooh is certain he will be lost without his friend by his side. As Pooh's creator, Christopher Robin doesn't want him to be afraid, but to have confidence. Through his abiding love for Pooh, he reminds the little bear that he possesses far more courage, strength, and intelligence than he realizes.

Often in life we lack faith in our own abilities. But we, too, have a creator who loves us and believes that we can do it. And it's OK for us to lean on the creator's love and light to reach our goals. Whatever it is that you aspire to achieve, believe it can happen. Know that the presence of love is always there to encourage and empower you.

Remember you are made in the image and likeness of the creator – therefore nothing can defeat or stop you. For, as we are told in Romans 8:37, *'In all these things we are more than conquerors through him who loved us.'* (NIV)

To learn more about Keith Magee, see page 4.

GOD IS ALWAYS PROTECTING YOU

By Helen Berry

The Lord watches over you –
        the Lord is your shade at your right hand;
the sun will not harm you by day,
        nor the moon by night.

Psalm 121:5-6 (NIV)

After you awake in the morning how long does it take before the anxieties of the day crowd in? A few seconds? A few minutes? I know I occasionally get overwhelmed at the start of the day, especially listening to the news, or if I know I've got to deal with something hard at work.

Every day is an 'ascent' – we climb mountains sometimes even before breakfast. Everything can seem like an uphill struggle. Truth is, we hardly ever reach the summit, even when everything goes smoothly. But we've got to keep on trying to do our very best, day in, day out.

Take a moment, right now, to stop and imagine what it would be like to think God is right next to you all the way – as close as the shadow of your right hand. That shade God provides is powerful – the only shelter we can trust. What would it mean to live there always, without apprehension?

Why do we fear those mountains we have to climb so much? If God has promised that not even the sun, with its burning heat, can harm us, what do we really have left to be anxious about? The psalmist says the moon has no power to hurt us either, which means our night terrors are just our imagination running wild. Day or night, it's all the same – we are under God's unfailing protective cover.

Live fearlessly. God is always close. Be free knowing nothing can harm your soul – you are always in safe hands.

Helen Berry lives in Devon, UK and is a Professor of History at the University of Exeter and former Lay Minister with Northern Lights Metropolitan Community Church, Newcastle upon Tyne. She believes we are all loved and accepted by God without exception.

GOD WILL TRANSFORM YOUR SADNESS INTO JOY
By Jermaine and Sarah Myrie

… and provide for those who grieve in Zion—
to bestow on them a crown of beauty
>   *instead of ashes,*
the oil of joy
>   *instead of mourning,*
and a garment of praise
>   *instead of a spirit of despair.*
They will be called oaks of righteousness,
>   *a planting of the Lord*
>   *for the display of his splendor.*
>   Isaiah 61:3 (NIV)

Each moment in time contains two possibilities – either something positive or something negative may materialize from it. Naturally, we hope the outcome we are walking toward will be an improvement on whatever we are leaving behind, and so we try to move forward in a spirit of optimism. Yet we often feel unsure whether our steps really will take us to a better place. But faith, by definition, allows us to believe there truly *is* something good awaiting us on the other side of every experience – seen or unseen.

Isaiah 61:3 tells us our 'ashes' – the things we have grieved over and that have brought despair into our lives – are not settled realities within our stories. Instead, those ashes can be resurrected as something better than what we knew before. For in the Word, the Lord will turn what was once a crown of thorns into a crown of glory. When faith in God takes root in our hearts, righteousness and splendor emerge, even from what we think of as our dead moments.

So we say to you, don't mourn too long over that broken relationship, that job you didn't get, or that dream that failed to materialize. Like seedlings that grow in a burnt forest, God will bring beautiful and abundant new blessings into your life from the ashes you see around you today.

Jermaine and Sarah Myrie reside in Massachusetts, USA and are active in supporting various educational and civic causes that serve to make their community more equitable and inclusive.

GOD'S MENTAL WEIGHT-LOSS PROGRAM
By Barbara Reynolds

"Come to Me all you who labor and are heavy laden, and I will give you rest. Take My yoke upon you and learn from Me, for I am gentle and lowly in heart, and you will find rest for your souls. For My yoke is easy and My burden is light."

Matthew 11:28-30 (NKJV)

For years, I was a yo-yo dieter, up and down, trying to lose weight. You might say I was heavy laden. After many years of trying, I have finally almost reached my ideal weight. Victory is mine.

That was physical, but soon I had another weight problem. In my prayers, the Lord told me to defend Him against the audacity of some of His human creations who were constructing artificial humanoids made in the image not of the Lord, but of flawed men and women.

When I resolved to answer God's call, I knew nothing about artificial intelligence or robotics. It took me seven years to author a scholarly acceptable work.

Then, after struggling to find a suitable publisher, I couldn't afford to fund promotional activities. Sales of my book were flat.

For a while I was crushed. I had done what God wanted, but the results were disappointing. I felt overwhelmed, depressed, and burnt out. I experienced many sleepless nights until I began a spiritual and mental weight-loss program.

First, I had to remember our bodies are the temple of the Holy Spirit, so surely God knows and cares about what we are going through. I started to see I was not carrying this project alone – God was my partner. I began internalizing scriptures that advise us to trust in the Lord rather than lean on our own understanding (Proverbs 3:5) or that describe how God orders our footsteps (Proverbs 16:9). My anxiety gradually decreased.

Today, I no longer feel so heavy laden. I have learned that the more we rest in the power of God, the more miraculous our mental weight loss.

Barbara Reynolds is an award-winning author and journalist and an ordained reverend from Prince George's County, MD, USA. She believes we can all use our voice in the service of the Lord – we just need to recognize we have the agency to do so.

HEALING AND PEACE IN A TIME OF WAR
By Keith Magee

Jesus said, "It is not the healthy who need a doctor, but the sick."

Matthew 9:12 (NIV)

With this profound statement Jesus acknowledges both physical and spiritual healing. He understood that in times of pain and brokenness, healing is essential. He recognized the role of doctors and the importance of earthly remedies in restoring well-being. Today, as war ravages lands like Gaza, the need for healing – for both bodies and souls – is immense.

In a CNN Opinion piece, Palestinian-born and Yale-trained orthopedic surgeon Ali H. Elaydi reflects on the urgent need for trained doctors in Gaza. Dr. Elaydi highlights how the medical community is being blocked from offering life-saving care to his people, emphasizing that in the midst of conflict, medical care is not just a necessity, but a right. Without access to qualified physicians, the wounded are left without the treatment they need to survive.

Jesus' words remind us of the essential mission doctors fulfill in times of crisis, underscoring the duty to provide relief to those who are suffering.

War devastates both flesh and spirit, yet even in the darkest of times, the possibility of healing remains. In the Quran, Surah Ash-Shu'ara 26:80 says, '*And when I am ill, it is He who cures me.*' This verse speaks to the ultimate source of healing beyond human capacity, offering hope that even in the bleakest of circumstances, wholeness is possible.

In the face of destruction, let us strive for healing – both through medical care and the deep, restorative peace that comes from God.

To learn more about Keith Magee, see page 4.

IN WITH THE OLD, IN WITH THE NEW
By Garrick Wilson

Yahweh's tender mercies have no end, and the kindness of his endless love is never exhausted.

New, fresh mercies greet me with every sunrise.
                        Lamentations 3:22-23 (TPT)

You might be thinking, isn't the saying, "*Out* with the old, in with the new?"

While that's true, I chose the phrasing of this title intentionally. The traditional saying, often associated with our New Year's resolutions, reflects a tendency in our world to supplant the old with the new. Think of how often we replace our phones, not because they're broken, but because a more up-to-date model has hit the market. Moving forward and closing old chapters in our life can feel aspirational, because some things are "so last season," right?

But before you discard your old, let's pause and reflect. Lamentations 3:22-23 reminds us that God's mercies have no end. Could it be that what we consider "new" is really just the old revisited? God, the ancient one, does not upgrade or change, yet with each dawn His mercies are renewed, offering hope after the dark night.

If we were to imagine God's new mercies, what would they look like? Personally, I awake daily to the same well-known surroundings and people, including my beautiful wife. By intentionally seeing her with fresh eyes, she becomes newly familiar to me every morning. Maybe *'new, fresh mercies'* are less about *what* we see and more about *how* we see.

Lord, thank You for the gift of seeing the old through new eyes each day, a blessing made possible by Your timeless and unfailing mercy at every sunrise.

Garrick Wilson is an academic and thought leader residing in the UK. He is Senior Pastor of NTCG Covenant Church in Reading and believes in empowering people to rise.

INSIDER OR OUTSIDER: GOD GOES BEYOND OUR LABELS AND CATEGORIES

By Lenny López

So she fell on her face, bowed down to the ground, and said to him, "Why have I found favor in your eyes, that you should take notice of me, since I am a foreigner?"

Ruth 2:10 (NKJV)

The story of Ruth in the Hebrew Bible is one of journeys between two countries that saw each other as enemies – Israel and Moab. Due to a famine, Israelites Naomi, her husband, and their two sons leave Bethlehem in Judah to start a new life in Moab. Years pass; Naomi's husband dies and both sons marry Moabite women, one of whom is named Ruth. Eventually, the sons also die, leaving all three women widowed and impoverished. Uncertain of their future, Naomi decides to return to the country of her birth. Out of loyalty, Ruth chooses to accompany her mother-in-law, bravely leaving the safety of her homeland to travel to a foreign place full of danger. In Bethlehem, Naomi and Ruth survive thanks to the kindness of an apparent stranger, Boaz, who allows Ruth to collect leftover crops from barley fields after harvesting.

Ultimately, Ruth is accepted into the community, marries Boaz, and has children who become the descendants of King David, the greatest king of Israel. God chooses a despised foreigner to be the bloodline for the monarchy, upending the notion that He values ethnic and religious purity for His kingdom. By centering a migration story of hunger, bereavement, isolation, and hard work, the Book of Ruth reminds us of the struggles faced by many. Throughout the Bible, God calls us to prioritize and provide for the poor, widows, orphans, and the foreign sojourner. Through radical generosity, may our hearts love and accept those whom others view as outsiders in our society.

Lenny López is a physician and health policy researcher who lives in San Francisco, CA, USA. His life's guiding principle is to do justice, to love kindness, and to walk humbly with God and others.

KNOW YOUR WHY
By Michael Wilson

I sat alone because your hand was on me.
Jeremiah 15:17 (NLT)

"Is there something wrong with me?"

I can't be the only person who has asked this. As human beings, we are hardwired to connect with others. And yet, there are times that require isolation from us, and that can leave us wondering how we fit in.

The prophet Jeremiah had a unique calling that set him apart and prevented him from marrying and having children. Despite his close connection to God, he is referred to as the "Weeping Prophet," reminding us that serving the Lord does not stop a person experiencing sadness and loneliness. Much as he loved his creator, Jeremiah was probably also inwardly conflicted.

When I compare my life with that of others, it is uniquely and sometimes painfully different. Perhaps you feel the same. But remember, Psalm 139:14 (ESV) tells us we are *'fearfully and wonderfully made'* – there is no-one on earth exactly like you. So instead of asking whether there is something wrong with you, seek to understand your WHY.

Why are you isolated? Why did your life not turn out as you planned? Why do you have a sense that you have a higher mission than most people?

God's hand is on you. He is always there to guide you through challenging circumstances and help you find answers to tough questions. If you are lonely, know that God often isolates us for a powerful purpose. That purpose may not shield you from difficult emotions, but identifying it should help direct you into divine wisdom.

And no – there is absolutely nothing wrong with you.

From Seneca, SC, USA, Michael Wilson is an ordained minister who walks in the prophetic calling. He is currently completing a Master's degree in counselling and rehabilitation.

LEARNING FORGIVENESS THROUGH LOSS
By Ameer Baraka

For the wages of sin is death, but the gift of God is eternal life in Christ Jesus our Lord.

Romans 6:23 (NIV)

Learning that I was going to be a father was the most incredible news. Everyone in my family had children except me, and in that moment, I felt a deep, joyful fulfillment. But that joy turned to rage when I discovered the child's mother had decided to end the pregnancy without my knowledge. It shattered me, leaving a wound I couldn't escape.

I struggled with anger and regret, especially as I looked back on my choices – how I'd been caught up in the lust of the flesh, ignoring the potential consequences. Yet, even in my brokenness, I found a place to stand in God's word. Romans 6:23 helped me remember that, though my sin had brought pain, God's love brings healing and forgiveness. Through this journey, I found the strength not just to forgive her, but also to forgive myself. I was able to let go of the bitterness, knowing God's mercy is new every morning.

Forgiveness opens a door to restore your heart. It also deepens your faith, as you come to understand every day is a chance to build stronger, truer relationships with God and the people He has put in your life. Forgiveness isn't easy, but it's powerful. And each new day is a reminder that God is with us, guiding us toward love and a deeper purpose.

Ameer Baraka is an Emmy nominated and award-winning actor from New Orleans, LA, USA. He has an unswerving faith in God and stands unapologetically on His word in spirit and truth.

MOTHERHOOD, IMPERFECTION, AND LOVE
By Carla Ortiz

"Yes, Mother. I can see you are flawed. You have not hidden it. That is your greatest gift to me."
Alice Walker, *Possessing the Secret of Joy*

As a mother, I know I am not without my faults. I have made mistakes, and I haven't hidden them from my children. They see my imperfections because I've never pretended to be anything other than human. I love my sons and daughters fiercely, sometimes with a sternness that they may not always understand, but it comes from a place of wanting to guide and protect them. Still, there are times I don't get it right – times when I've spoken too harshly or missed what they truly needed. In those moments, I've learned to apologize, to show them that love isn't about being perfect, but about being real and willing to grow. My vulnerability is not a weakness but a gift I give them, showing that even as adults, we are still learning.

Through my imperfections, I hope my children see the importance of grace, forgiveness, and humility.

And when I fall short, I trust they can find comfort not only in my love but in the deeper love that embraces us all.

As Isaiah 66:13 (ESV) says, '*As one whom his mother comforts, so I will comfort you.*' May my children always know that whether through my arms or God's, they are held in love.

Carla Ortiz is the mother of four adult children, three grandchildren, and many others who find home in her loving arms. She lives in South Jersey, NJ, USA.

MY DAILY PRAYER FOR PEACE IN TROUBLED TIMES
By Caroline Cracraft

"Who then is this, that even the wind and the sea obey him?"

Mark 4:41 (ESV)

In these troubled times, when the lives of so many people around the globe are impacted by the tragedy of war, I often reflect on this verse. It reminds us that Christ's early followers were in awe of His ability to quell the most violent tempest. Like them, we must recognize Jesus' divine authority and trust in Him to bring calm to even the most terrifying and chaotic of circumstances.

Each day when I wake, the first thing I do is offer praise and thanks to my Lord and brother, Jesus. I thank Him for the many blessings He has bestowed on me, such as my health and my wonderful family.

Then my thoughts quickly turn to all those who are so much less fortunate than I am.

I pray the Lord will bring an end to all the conflicts currently afflicting the world and allow the warring parties to find peace and reconciliation.

I pray He will bring relief to all those who suffer from physical or emotional pain, and to all those who are frightened or grieving, wherever they may be.

I pray God will help all the nations on earth come together to do what it takes to stop climate change and save our planet from our own destructive folly.

And I never lose hope that my prayers will be answered, for I know the power of faith can carry us through any storm.

Caroline Cracraft is a retired British vice-consul who lives in Chicago, IL, USA. For over three decades she was a member of the altar guild at St. Chrysostom's, where her acts of service were rooted in the pursuit of equality and justice.

OUT OF PAIN COME FAITHFULNESS AND HOPE
By Kipp Mann Benn

The steadfast love of the Lord never ceases;
*   his mercies never come to an end;*
they are new every morning;
*   great is your faithfulness.*

                    Lamentations 3:22-24 (ESV)

Lamentations 3:22-24 calls on readers to remember the constancy of the Lord's love. However, the context in which these words were written serves as an equally important reminder of the true nature of faith and hope.

The Book of Lamentations is traditionally believed to have been written by the prophet Jeremiah in the wake of the fall of Jerusalem around the 6th century BCE. The poems, therefore, come not from a place of happiness, but one of deep pain and sorrow. Indeed, in the text immediately preceding these verses, the author bemoans the terrible destruction, loss, and misery wrought on his city.

It is commonplace to think of faith and hope as intangible, almost magical phenomena. But their manifestation is not fantastical and remote, nor is it always joyful and positive. While faith in God's mercies may feel transcendent, it is not – it is robust and resolute, born out of the suffering of life.

When your faith is tested and your hope deflated, know this is exactly the course of the Lord's love. In such moments you must remind yourself that 'great faithfulness' is not always delicate and subtle, but often shows up as fortitude and grit as it rises once more. Take comfort in the knowledge that every morning brings the chance for a new beginning.

Kipp Mann Benn is a Magdalen College-Oxford Graduate Scholar at the University of Oxford, UK, reading for an MSc in Global Governance and Diplomacy. He believes strongly in the pursuit of prudential value through public service in order to help others.

REMEMBER TO SAY "THANK YOU"

By Keith Magee

In every thing give thanks: for this is the will of God in Christ Jesus concerning you.

1 Thessalonians 5:18 (KJV)

In the most trying moments of life, it can be easy to forget to say "thank you." Yet, those two simple words are one of the greatest gifts God has given us. This passage from Thessalonians reminds us to give thanks *in* everything, not *for* everything. God doesn't ask us to be thankful for pain, but He does call on us to find gratitude, even in the midst of it.

Each morning, my son Zayden and I remind ourselves, "Every day might not be a good day, but there's something good in every day." We also say that the difference between God and good is just the number of "o's." On some days that "something good" is hard to see, but it's unfailingly present – a warm conversation, a moment of peace, the kiss of grace, or the simple fact that we made it through. Gratitude is a lifeline; it shifts our focus from what is wrong to what is still right. It doesn't change our circumstances, but it can change our hearts.

We can learn from the story of the ten lepers in Luke 17:11-19. After Jesus healed them, only one returned to thank Him. Jesus noticed this act of gratitude, reminding us how precious it is to remember to say "thank you."

Let us always seek to be like the leper who found the time to give thanks to the one who healed and made him complete. For there is always something to be grateful for.

To learn more about Keith Magee, see page 4.

RETHINKING OUR EXPECTATIONS OF GOD

By Joseph Montgomery

Now when John [the Baptist] in prison heard about the activities of Christ, he sent word by his disciples and asked Him, "Are You the Expected One (the Messiah), or should we look for someone else [who will be the promised One]?"

Matthew 11:2-3 (AMP)

Indisputably the forerunner and baptizer of Jesus, John the Baptist was imprisoned for challenging King Herod's moral authority. When he was not freed, John questioned whether Christ was indeed the expected savior.

In his doubting, I believe John was in two different prisons at the same time: one belonged to King Herod and the other was a mental prison John built in his own mind. A mental prison exists when we are governed by our personal assumptions about what God is supposed to do.

Jesus performed miracles in front of John's disciples and sent them to report what they had witnessed. Hence, Jesus proved He was doing what He came to do: fulfilling prophecy, not preferences.

What if God does not meet our expectations because He intends to exceed them?

While my father was dying my thoughts were like those of John: "I am faithful Jesus, but my expectations are not being met." It was not that my belief in God's ability to heal had waivered. But I kept saying, "What are You waiting for? Heal him. There he is. Now is the time."

The Holy Spirit responded clearly: "Your dad is going to be healed, but not in the way you envisage."

To free myself from my mental prison, I set my expectations based on who Jesus truly is. I was reminded that the Lord might not organize events to match my preferences, but I believed – and still believe – in His omniscience. Blessed are they who accept without question what God is doing in their lives.

Joseph Montgomery has earned a Doctor of Jurisprudence. He is also an ordained minister and a native of Fredericksburg, VA, USA. He believes there ain't no mountain high enough to keep love and grace from transforming your life.

THE HEART OF AN INTERCESSOR
By Beverly Jackson

If you find it in your heart to care for somebody else, you will have succeeded.
Maya Angelou, *Wouldn't Take Nothing for My Journey Now*

As an intercessor, I find that caring for others is at the heart of what I do. Intercessory prayer is a sacred, often hidden act of love. It's a call to step into someone else's struggle and lift them before God, even when they don't know you're doing it. The beauty of intercession is that it doesn't seek recognition; it's done in the quiet moments, in the private corners of our lives, where only God sees.

I have come to realize that my gift from God is a calling not to public preaching but to private prayer. This calling is no less important, for prayer is the key that unlocks the door to God's answers. When I pray for others – whether for healing, guidance, or peace – I trust God is working behind the scenes in ways I may never witness. And that is enough, because prayer is not about being seen or heard by others; it is about bringing the needs of the world to God with a heart full of love.

The apostle Paul reminds us in 1 Timothy 2:1-2 (NIV), *'I urge, then, first of all, that petitions, prayers, intercession and thanksgiving be made for all people.'* As intercessors, we are called to care for others in the most profound way – by praying for them, trusting that God hears, and knowing that He answers.

A native Bostonian, Beverly Jackson has a career in a law firm and as a church administrator and is the lead intercessor for her pastor. She trusts that if you pray 'without ceasing' (1 Thessalonians 5:17; ESV), you can live in immeasurable peace.

THE MERCIES OF OUR MOTHERS
By Freddie Lee Burwell

And he said unto his father, My head, my head. And he said to a lad, Carry him to his mother.

2 Kings 4:19 (KJV)

There is no earthly degree of mercy that could compare to the mercies of God other than the mercies of our mothers. Just as Christ loves us unconditionally, so do our mothers. Our very conception occurred in the womb of our mother, just as the conception of the Son of God occurred in the womb of the Blessed Virgin Mary. So why is it women are still treated as "less than"?

In 2 Kings 4:19 a Shunammite woman's son is out working in the hot sun with his father. When the son takes ill in the fields, complaining of severe head pain, his father has one of the other workers carry him back home to his mother. She gently nurtures the boy until he dies and then after death is carried unto the prophet Elisha and brought back to life. A mother will stick with her child through thick and thin up unto the very end, and then some.

Let us strive to recognize the true value of our mothers and of all women. May we never forget the contributions of the likes of Reverend Mother Sojourner Truth, Moms Mabley, Mother Teresa, Queen Elizabeth the Queen Mother, and the "Big Mamas" of all our families.

Let us pray that intellectual, spiritual, and merciful women – such as "Mamala" Kamala Harris – will forever remain steadfast, unmovable, and always abounding in the work of the Lord as leaders of a free and equal world.

Freddie Lee Burwell is a USA Associate Minister of Greater Mt. Calvary Holy Church in Washington, DC, USA, where he lives. He believes we are all the children of God by faith in Christ Jesus.

THE POWER OF PRAYER
By James Grout

Do not be anxious about anything, but in everything by prayer and supplication with thanksgiving let your requests be made known to God. And the peace of God, which surpasses all understanding, will guard your hearts and your minds in Christ Jesus.

Philippians 4:6-7 (ESV)

Have you ever felt overwhelmed by the chaos of life, as if your worries were a relentless tide? In Philippians 4:6-7, the apostle Paul invites us into a profound sanctuary of tranquillity, urging us not to be anxious but to present our requests to God. This promise resonates deeply – it is not merely the absence of worry, but a divine peace that transcends our comprehension.

As we embark on this journey, we must recognize the transformative power of prayer. In our moments of distress, turning our thoughts to God can shift our perspective from fear to faith. Paul encourages us to bring everything before God – our struggles, our hopes, our fears. This act of surrender is not passive; it is an active choice to trust in God's sovereignty.

The promise of peace is not contingent upon our circumstances. It is rooted in the character of God, who is ever-present and infinitely wise. When we entrust our worries to Him, we open ourselves to His peace, which guards our hearts and minds. This divine protection allows us to navigate life's storms with a calm assurance, knowing we are held in His loving embrace.

Today, take a moment to reflect on what weighs heavily on your heart. Bring those concerns before God in prayer, opening your soul to His serenity. Let this be a reminder that in the midst of turmoil, the peace of God is a steadfast anchor. Embrace this gift, and let it transform your life.

James Grout is a final-year undergraduate student at Durham University in the UK. He is inspired by the message that through prayer God's peace is always available to everyone, regardless of their circumstances.

THE WISDOM OF SELF-CARE
By Tracie D. Hall

Every wise woman builds her house,
*   but the foolish one tears it down with her own hands.*

Proverbs 14:1 (WEB)

When I first encountered this verse, I was immediately struck by how it seemed to underscore the importance of women's agency and independence.

That spoke to me. As a young woman growing up in a tough neighborhood, I'd made it my goal to pursue a career that would provide financial stability, to give back to my community, and to make a mark on the world.

I was going to build my own house!

Years flew by as I worked a succession of demanding jobs, served on boards and committees, and supported members of my family through illness and death.

It wasn't until I sat in the doctor's office facing a list of check-engine lights that I realized I had failed to heed the second part of Proverbs 14:1.

In my determination to raise my house alone (and to help everyone around me raise theirs too), I'd neglected to ask for help when I needed it. I'd neglected to rest. I'd neglected to allow myself to fully grieve loved ones. I'd stopped checking on my health and well-being.

If my house was being torn down, it was by my own doing.

That afternoon, with my physician's warning in my ear, I vowed to make changes. Gradually, I began to reduce the number of commitments I balanced and relationships I carried without reciprocity. I even altered how I approached my professional life.

It's still a work in progress, but my house feels lighter and happier now. And I've learned I don't have to maintain it all by myself.

With a career encompassing library and arts administration, the private sector, philanthropy, and higher education, Tracie D. Hall divides her time between Chicago, IL, Montgomery, AL, and Seattle, WA, USA. She believes each of us possesses genius that should be nurtured and shared.

WALKING IN THE CREATOR'S ACCEPTANCE
By Alisha Lola Jones and Calvin Taylor Skinner

The Lord your God is in your midst,
*   a warrior who gives victory;*
he will rejoice over you with gladness,
*   he will renew you in his love;*
he will exult over you with loud singing.
                                Zephaniah 3:17 (RSV)

How do we remain spiritually balanced in an isolating digital culture centered on approval through 'likes,' 'follows,' and virtual friendships? We find solace in the fact that we are already accepted by the one who created us. The prophet Zephaniah reminds us of God's unwavering presence and joy in who we are as His beloved, and calls us to return to the Lord whenever we feel overwhelmed by the demands of life.

Zephaniah assures us, '*He will rejoice over you with gladness, he will renew you in his love.*' Imagine a God who delights in singing over you! God's song addresses our fears, renews our spirits, and invites us into the creator's grace. As we reflect

59

on God's faithfulness – from the Emancipation Proclamation to modern movements for justice – we find encouragement to work for what is just and right.

Walking in the creator's acceptance requires depending on God in every action. We must embody self-awareness and compassion as we engage with others. Let us not grow weary in serving those in need, for in doing so, we reflect God's love. We are called to promote balance through core behaviors. These include helping the vulnerable without hesitation; gathering in community to support one another; and maintaining spiritual practices and key values even amidst turmoil.

Lord, thank You for singing over us in jubilation. In our weariness, may we find strength in Your presence and courage in Your promises. Help us to serve, pray, and love boldly, trusting that You are with us every step of the way. Amen.

Alisha Lola Jones is an associate professor in the faculty of music at the University of Cambridge, UK. As an ordained minister, she is dedicated to harnessing sacred music to help people discover their life rhythm. Calvin Taylor Skinner is a minister, activist, and community organizer based in both Cambridge, UK, and Knoxville, TN, USA. He believes in the power of community, advocacy, and the amplification of marginalized voices to inspire meaningful change.

WE ARE BLESSED TO KNOW CEASELESS LOVE
By Gloria Ampadu-Darko

The steadfast love of the Lord never ceases;
       his mercies never come to an end;
they are new every morning;
       great is your faithfulness.
                              Lamentations 3:22-24 (ESV)

I can't help but groan when I notice the 26-minutes-and-30-seconds time stamp on a new voice message from my mother. I brace myself before I realize such an extended voice message is none other than a recording of her nightly devotionals. Despite the length, the tenderness and care that radiate from such messages are a reminder that nothing will prevent my mother from connecting with me. Undeterred by the many miles that separate us, she continues a sacred ritual that was part of our bedtime routine during my childhood. As I listen to her recite her chosen scriptures for the night, I have no doubt that her love never ceases. In a way, I feel it renewed with the arrival of each message.

For many, there is a perceived distance from the Lord, whether it be the physical separation between heaven and earth or the spiritual distance experienced by those who, like me, are uncertain in their faith journey. Such distance sometimes makes it difficult to recognize the unwavering love of God. Yet, despite this, He always ensures that His love is bestowed upon us. Even when we worry our blessings have stalled, that is never the case. God's love is unconditional, and His mercies are limitless. Even when our flawed humanity makes us slow to perceive and accept it, His love renews day in and day out. Simply put, we are blessed and highly favored.

Gloria Ampadu-Darko, a Boston University alumna and Deloitte Consulting analyst based in Washington, DC, in the USA, lives by the belief that celebrating cultural diversity fosters meaningful connections and strengthens communities.

WHEN A FRIEND BECOMES A BROTHER
By Zayden Magee

"Oh no! These facts and opinions look so similar!"
Joy, *Inside Out* by Pixar Animation Studios

From the outside, my best friend and I may not look very alike. But from the moment we met, we became more than just friends – we became brothers. Even though I'm from an African-American family and my friend has Italian and Pakistani-American heritage, we don't see the differences. We see what really matters: we both love Lego, watching *Slugterra*, and playing *Roblox* and *Minecraft*. We laugh, share stories, and imagine whole new worlds together.

Proverbs 18:24 tells us a friend can stick closer than a brother. And that's true for us. Sometimes the world sees us as different, but in our hearts, we know we're the same. We both want to have fun, be kind, and feel safe. When we're together, we forget about what makes us look different on the outside because we know that true love and friendship are bigger than anything else.

Just like Joy says in *Inside Out*, facts and opinions often look similar. But we know that the facts about our differences don't matter as much as our opinions – because to us, friendship is what truly matters. I hope every child knows the love of a friend, and even more, the love of God, who made us all special, yet equal.

Zayden Magee is ten years old and lives in the UK with his father who helped him to write these words.

WHICH WAY SHOULD I GO, LORD?
By Rob and Kem Greene

And though the Lord give you the bread of adversity and the water of affliction, yet your Teacher will not hide himself anymore, but your eyes shall see your Teacher. And your ears shall hear a word behind you, saying, "This is the way, walk in it," when you turn to the right or when you turn to the left.

Isaiah 30:20-21 (ESV)

Have you ever wondered "What do I do now?" or "Where am I going?" A big decision is ahead of you and you're not sure how to make it. Or maybe after making a choice you're not sure if you've made the correct one.

Both of us have read this passage from Isaiah many times thinking it was saying God would tell us whether to go right or left down 'Decision Street.' Maybe if we really focused on Him, He would tell us what to do.

Then one day something was highlighted to Rob. The Lord wasn't telling him what to do, He was doing something much more comforting! The option of choosing 'right *or* left' made Robert realize the choice wasn't really the point. Now we understand this scripture more like this: after some adversity we will see and hear God. We'll hear Him saying, "You're going the right way," regardless of which way we choose!

How can this be? It's because, as believers, the Lord wants us to know that *who* we make the decision with is much more important than *what* decision is made. He is the one who works all things together for our good!

When making decisions today, remember the Lord is with you. When you see and hear Him, it's impossible for you to go the wrong way. You can trust Him with your choices!

Rob and Kem Greene are ministers of the gospel, dividing their time between the USA, UK, and Nigeria. Newly married, they believe in the wisdom of Proverbs 3:5 – trusting in the Lord and not leaning on your own understanding will direct your path into all of His promises.

AFTERTHOUGHT

What makes this collection of 31 reflections unique is the transparency and thoughtfulness of its contributors, who share openly from their personal journeys. They each bring a piece of their lives – moments of joy and pain, questioning and revelation, victory and struggle – allowing us to witness the powerful intersection of faith and human experience. Through these honest accounts, the writers offer comfort and inspiration. They invite us to find courage in our own stories and to know that we are never alone in our victories or our struggles.

In a world in which looking after ourselves can feel like an overwhelming task, these narratives show that spiritual and mental health are not only compatible but essential to a balanced, fulfilling life. Faith and mental health support go hand in hand, enabling us to face challenges with resilience and serenity. For there is a wellspring of strength available to us when we live with both a profound, meaningful belief in God and intentional care for our emotional well-being. As the scripture says, '*I wish above all things that thou mayest prosper and be in health, even as thy soul prospereth*' (3 John 2;

KJV), this devotional calls us to nurture our body, mind, and spirit.

My hope is that as you close this book, planning to revisit it often, you feel a rejuvenated sense of purpose and encouragement for what lies ahead. Life may not promise us endless good days, but this collection assures us that there is something good to be found in every day – a small blessing, a quiet joy, a touch of grace.

May these be anchoring truths and gentle reminders that you are not only seen but deeply loved, and that, indeed, God's mercies are new every morning.

Keith Magee

ACKNOWLEDGMENTS

This collection would not have been possible without the generous contributors who all said "yes" without hesitation. I am deeply grateful to each of you for helping to manifest this source of hope, inspiration, and wisdom. Words cannot fully express how my spirit leaped when "Dr. Robin" welcomed this book into her heart and spirit, graciously agreeing to write the Foreword. My heartfelt thanks to Joanne Clay for her editorial genius and invaluable guidance. I remain appreciative of Bruce Bobbins for continuing to ensure my voice is amplified. I am grateful for David Ziyambi's sound legal counsel. I am also indebted to Tyra Enchill and Beverly Jackson for their unwavering support.

I often quote Maya Angelou, who said, "I come as one, but I stand as ten thousand." To all of you who stand with me, I am immensely grateful – especially to my mother, Barbara Reynolds, and "Mum C" Caroline Cracraft. To my adored son Zayden, the most important person in the world to me. To the Berachah Family, a virtual community of believers where I'm allowed to continue to practice my faith as not your normal pastor, because they are not a normal church – you provide the undergirding strength and prayers that keep me grounded, and I am honored to serve you.

To my father, the late Alvin Magee, who saw me before I understood myself and trusted that I would soar to places beyond his imagination, I dedicate this work with profound love and gratitude.

And to you, the reader – this collection gains significance because you chose to pick it up. For that, I am, and we are, deeply thankful.

Keith Magee

CONTRIBUTORS

Alexa and Paul Achkar

Gloria Ampadu-Darko

Ameer Baraka

Helen Berry

Bryan Bonaparte

Freddie Lee Burwell

Caroline Cracraft

Cyntoria Grant

Rob and Kem Greene

James Grout

Tracie D. Hall

Beverly Jackson

Théo Le Douarin

Lenny López

Keith Magee

Zayden Magee

Kipp Mann Benn

Joseph Montgomery

Valerie Mosley

Monica Murray

Jermaine and Sarah Myrie

Carla Ortiz

Barbara Reynolds

Alisha Lola Jones and
Calvin Taylor Skinner

Michael Turton

Sharon White

Garrick Wilson

Michael Wilson

Printed in the USA
CPSIA information can be obtained
at www.ICGtesting.com
LVHW070206101224
798688LV00053B/1675